Based on the best-selling piano method by Kenneth Baker.

THE COMPLETE PIANO PLAYER
RACHMANINOFF

Wise Publications
London/New York/Paris/Sydney/Copenhagen/Berlin/Madrid/Hong Kong/Tokyo

Exclusive distributors:
Music Sales Limited
14-15 Berners Street,
London W1T 3LJ, UK.
Music Sales Pty Limited
Units 3-4, 17 Willfox Street, Condell Park
NSW 2200, Australia.

This book © Copyright 2014 by Wise Publications.
Order No. AM1009140
ISBN: 978-1-78305-617-0

Arranged by Barrie Carson Turner.
Processed by Paul Ewers Music Design.
Edited by Ruth Power.

Printed in the EU.

Your Guarantee of Quality
As publishers, we strive to produce every book to the
highest commercial standards.
This book has been carefully designed to minimise awkward page turns
and to make playing from it a real pleasure.
Particular care has been given to specifying acid-free, neutral-sized
paper made from pulps which have not been elemental chlorine bleached.
This pulp is from farmed sustainable forests and was produced with
special regard for the environment.
Throughout, the printing and binding have been planned to ensure a sturdy,
attractive publication which should give years of enjoyment.
If your copy fails to meet our high standards, please
inform us and we will gladly replace it.

www.musicsales.com

7 Morceaux de salon, Op.10
VI. Romance

Composed by Sergei Rachmaninoff

Andante

Aleko
XI. Intermezzo

Composed by Sergei Rachmaninoff

Allegretto pastorale

Élégie
No.1 from 'Morceaux de Fantasie', Op.3

Composed by Sergei Rachmaninoff

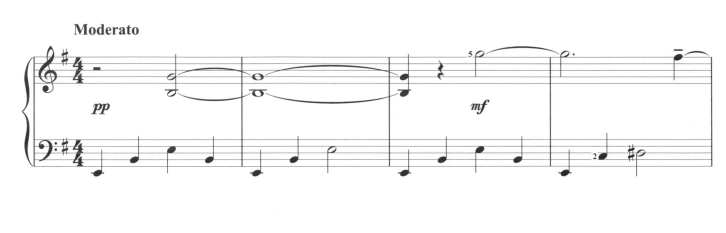

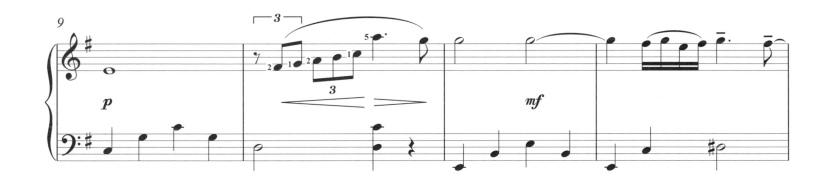

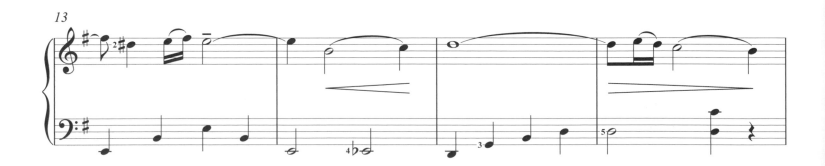

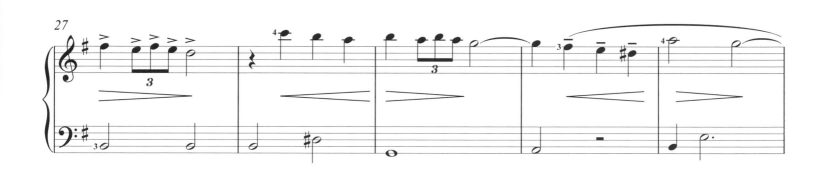

Fragments
II-19-3

Composed by Sergei Rachmaninoff

Piano Concerto No.2
1st Movement

Composed by Sergei Rachmaninoff

poco meno mosso   **rit.**

14

Piano Concerto No.2
2nd Movement

Composed by Sergei Rachmaninoff

Adagio sostenuto

Piano Concerto No.3
1st Movement

Composed by Sergei Rachmaninoff

Piano Sonata No. 1
1st Movement

Composed by Sergei Rachmaninoff

Allegro moderato

Piano Sonata No.2, Op.36
2nd Movement

Composed by Sergei Rachmaninoff

Prélude
No.2 from 'Morceaux de Fantasie', Op.3

Composed by Sergei Rachmaninoff

Preludes, Op.23
V. Alla marcia

Composed by Sergei Rachmaninoff

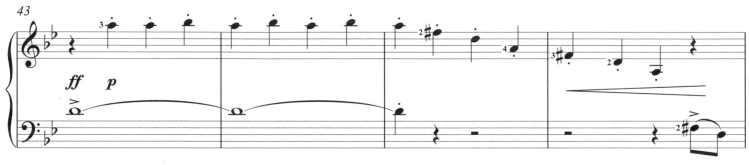

Tempo primo

Preludes, Op. 23
X. Largo

Composed by Sergei Rachmaninoff

Original key: G♭ major

Largo ♩ = 50

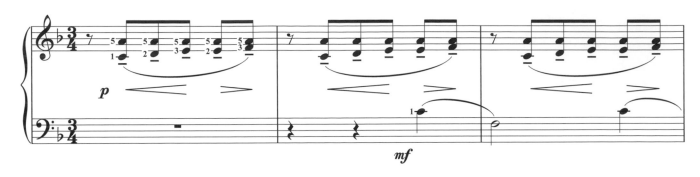

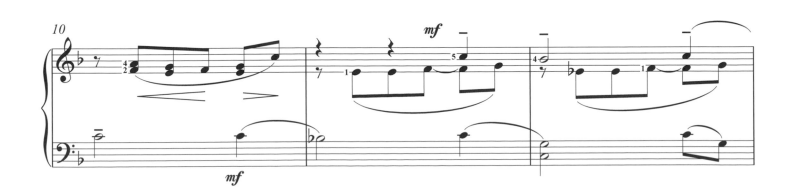

poco a poco cresc. ed accel.

Preludes, Op.32
V. Moderato

Composed by Sergei Rachmaninoff

Rhapsody On A Theme Of Paganini

Composed by Sergei Rachmaninoff

Theme
Allegro vivace

Var. XVIII

Lento, poco rubato ♩ = c.50

Symphonic Dances
1st Movement

Composed by Sergei Rachmaninoff

Non Allegro ♩ = 114

Symphony No.2
3rd Movement

Composed by Sergei Rachmaninoff

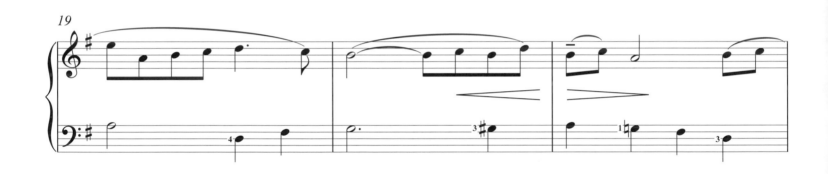

Vocalise
No. 14 from 'Fourteen Songs', Op.34

Composed by Sergei Rachmaninoff

123456789